STEVEN GAMBREL

STEVEN GAMBREL
PERSPECTIVE

PHOTOGRAPHY BY ERIC PIASECKI

RIZZOLI
NEW YORK

New York · Paris · London · Milan

CONTENTS

INTRODUCTION

Since the publication of my first book, *Steven Gambrel: Time and Place*, in 2012, I have had many wonderful opportunities to pour myself into the myriad details that make projects feel special and unique. My team thrives on these projects. We love mock-ups, new wares, and novel combinations of true-and-tested materials. Our perennial quest is to reinterpret tradition with intriguing twists and irreverent juxtapositions. It takes a willing and fearless client to be open to such creative explorations. Happily, I have found that when I push the limits and present an idea in the abstract, I usually get positive feedback.

It is still crucially important to me that our design for each space draws inspiration from local references and resonates with the character of the building and the evolving sensibilities of the current owner, particularly since we often work with the same client multiple times. I remind clients that ideas and inspiration are infinite, waiting to be discovered on every travel adventure and site visit. The particular charm of a streetscape in one city can set the tone for the next project. Neighborhoods, building materials, vistas, and the client's perspective all meld to form the initial design concept. Right from the start, the owner's decision to acquire the property gives me a lot of insight into what he or she is trying to achieve. In the end, a new local vernacular develops, representing the individual who inhabits the space and the changing spirit of the place.

TOWN

PALMOLIVE BUILDING APARTMENT

CHICAGO

In 2015, a Chicago couple asked me to review plans for a full-floor apartment they had recently bought in a handsome, historically significant building with spectacular views of Lake Michigan. The clients intended the apartment to be primarily for their private use, with space for occasional guests and entertaining. Their sophisticated art collection and personal style encouraged me to believe they would be open to complex color combinations and rich layering of materials. The strong reflective light from the lake, weighty massing of historic buildings in every view, and the city's urban rigor suggested a strong masculine palette. I recommended collaborating with the very talented Chicago-based firm Liederbach & Graham Architects, with whom we had recently completed a successful project in nearby Lincoln Park. During my visits to Chicago, Phil Liederbach and Michael Graham took me to see the elegant 1928 art deco Casino Club and gave me a superb tour of David Adler houses and historic streets to savor classic Chicago. During that time together, we discovered our shared interest in the minutest details.

Project meetings began with initial schemes presented in my office that incorporated terrazzo samples, fumed oak, muted Venetian plasters, and rich woods to evoke Chicago high style. The textiles and overall palette were derived from the seemingly infinite gray-blueness of Lake Michigan. The highlight of our scheme was a saddle-stitched leather library inspired by Frances Elkins and David Adler. It was a direct homage to the design duo's famous library for the circa 1929 Kersey Coates Reed House in Lake Forest, Illinois, arguably one of the most beautiful rooms of the twentieth century. Elkins and Adler had chosen to work with a pale, warm, neutral leather, as mellow as the books in the room. I planned to echo this, until we all became captivated by a leather sample that was deep red, supple, and complex. It was so strikingly opposed to our initial lake-inspired scheme that we knew we had landed on a twisted urban artifice—something that makes working in cities such a delight.

A vintage LaVerne console stands in the vestibule. FOLLOWING SPREAD: The view from the entrance is enfilade, ending with a fireplace and an Italian Murano mirror.

Fumed oak floors were custom made for the apartment. OPPOSITE: In the living room, a high-gloss ceiling reflects light from Lake Michigan. The walls, which are waxed and polished Venetian plaster, add to the ethereal palette and amplify the light that filters through the space. The large painting is by Bridget Riley. FOLLOWING SPREAD: The 1961 painting is by Francisco Bores; the molded glass mantel was custom made for the room.

An orange-red 1930s French cabinet sets the tone for the living room. Lighting is 1950s Italian by FontanaArte, and the painting is by Frank Auerbach. OPPOSITE: The slender one-of-a-pair vitrine is lined in red velvet and filled with a collection of bronze sculptures, including pieces by Danish craftsman Just Andersen. FOLLOWING SPREAD: The saddle-stitched red leather library has a Belgian Rouge Griotte mantel.

PREVIOUS SPREAD AND ABOVE: The custom dining table has inserted eglomise tops to reflect the lake. The chairs are a set by Jean-Michel Frank. The enfilade ends with the leather library, concealed behind a pair of mercury-mirrored, Harmon-hinged rosewood doors. Vitrines are bedecked with art books and a collection of 1950s Danish porcelains. OPPOSITE: Phillip Liederbach designed the marble mantel; he also devised the elaborate paneling and jib door leading to the apartment's private quarters.

The red library called for a unique stitched paneling to provide contrast to the more elaborate paneling of the nearby painted rooms. I gently infused hints of red into the smallest details throughout the apartment and introduced a sumptuous orange-red lacquered 1930s French cabinet. In Paris, we discovered a set of Jean-Michel Frank–designed dining chairs that were covered in crusty original oxblood leather. This further imbued color into the enfilade of public spaces. The John Staub–inspired doors, veneered in exotic Makassar rosewood and inset with antiqued mirror slivers, complement the reddish tones and add a sense of urban luxe that has been interpreted to exquisite effect in many settings—from the Doge's Palace in Venice to English Georgian manor houses—and never seems to go out of fashion.

In the kitchen, shelves flanking the hood are mounted on walls clad in large sheets of white milk glass. They display a collection of vintage hotel silver—one of my signature decorative elements.

Hotel silver. OPPOSITE: The banquette is reminiscent of upholstered seats in vintage cars made in Detroit. The ceiling is inspired by one I admired in the American Bar in Vienna, designed by Adolf Loos in 1903. The striped artwork is by Bridget Riley.

The master bathroom is a study in contrasting marbles and has subtle deco references rendered in bronze.

The long bedroom hall has a slightly barreled ceiling in waxed plaster, and the walls are clad with hand-textured plaster and bees-wax paper by Asterisk Designs. The vintage German lamps are Luzette pendants by Peter Behrens, originally made for factories in the 1930s. ABOVE: In the master bedroom, an art deco mantel is fashioned from Derbyshire Fossil limestone. The salon-style art hangs from chains and is illuminated by picture lights for a soft glow.

The office is between the master bedroom and the dressing room. It needed an identity so I designed the space to resemble vintage luggage, with bleached walnut straps and bark paper for texture. ABOVE: The dressing room cabinetry is made of American bleached walnut with deco fixtures that feel very Chicago.

FIFTH AVENUE DUPLEX

NEW YORK CITY

This elegant staircase is completely original, designed by McKim, Mead & White in 1912. We hired artisans to plaster the walls with scored lines to emulate stone, echoing the original limestone floors. The entry hall has an unusual mix of periods and styles: a mid-twentieth-century French iron console with Danish stools, an eighteenth-century Irish mirror, and an American lamp by William "Billy" Haines.

PREVIOUS SPREAD AND THIS SPREAD: Our design objective for the living room was to create a soothing space where refined pieces complement one another; nothing stands out except carefully curated artwork. The Billy Haines game table, fully clad in leather, was manufactured by Stergis in 1946.

The dining room's original paneling seemed fussy until we painted it deep blue and then added combed Venetian plaster panels. A high-gloss ceiling and a strong flame-stitched silk carpet enliven the room. We replaced the original mahogany doors with taller versions—a subtle change to emphasize the generous ceiling height.

On Fifth Avenue, a handful of grand historic residential buildings have coveted apartments with unparalleled proportions and architectural merit. I was delighted to be asked to renovate and redesign the interiors of a duplex where many of the original details were intact, but just enough parts were missing to make it possible to leave one's mark on an epic urban space. The 1912 building was designed by the renowned firm McKim, Mead & White in the guise of a Roman Renaissance palazzo. A majestic limestone entryway with a heavily detailed wrought-metal canopy leads to a polished limestone lobby, where a nineteenth-century Italian console was incorporated into the McKim design. The polished mahogany elevator rises to apartments heralded by perfectly preserved broad doorways.

The clients, a young couple with children, asked me to come up with something that would last a lifetime. We restored some of the opulent details, like the ironwork balustrade of the sweeping limestone staircase, and had the mahogany doors replicated a foot taller to emphasize the sumptuous scale of the large public spaces. (The smaller doors were reinstalled upstairs in the bedroom wing.) We divided the second large drawing room into two smaller spaces, creating a family sitting room and a pine-paneled office where the couple could work together in privacy. I lacquered the family room in a deep, rich peacock blue as a counterpoint to the waxed pine study. The living room retains its original painted paneling, which I chose to paint in four shades of gray, and the ceiling was given a high-gloss finish after many months of sanding and plastering. We collected twentieth-century furniture by eminent French and American designers to mix with custom upholstery and the clients' impressive contemporary art collection. In the dining room, the 1912 plaster overmantel, cornice, and marble mantel seemed a bit overwrought in their early twentieth-century ornamentation, but the deep-blue scheme and combed Venetian plasterwork made the room feel more lively and contemporary.

The black lacquered kitchen was custom designed with blocks of contrasting marble on the floor.

The high-gloss peacock-blue sitting room takes on a soothing atmosphere with a mix of various blue tones throughout. The club chairs are vintage Italian, by Paolo Buffa. FOLLOWING SPREAD: The mellow pine office is a study in multiple patterns. The owners work together at the partners' desk.

Ice-blue silk walls in the master bedroom are paired with warm wood tones and punctuated with silvered brass. The effect is calm and restful. ABOVE: In the master bathroom, slabs of pale Bleu de Savoie and dark Grigio Carnico marble are trimmed with generous quantities of nickel, which captures reflective light. Pale gray Venetian plaster melds the walls and marble slabs into a tranquil overall environment.

PARK AVENUE PREWAR

NEW YORK CITY

Large prewar Park Avenue apartments are a rare commodity. When offered the plum assignment to redesign this impressive space, lined with terraces and generously scaled rooms, I could easily imagine the materials and strong palette that would transform the classic proportions and breathe new life into the interiors. The couple had raised their children in a great old house on Long Island and was ready to move to Manhattan, settle into an apartment, and assemble an impressive art collection. They hired Gary Brewer, a partner with Robert A. M. Stern Architects, and we teamed up to personalize the space. Gary transformed the floor plan and devised architectural elements inspired by the building's handsome exterior, but with more ornamentation than had previously been present. I once read that during Park Avenue's building boom in the 1920s, the area rose so fast you could feel the humidity from all the drying plaster in the atmosphere. I was less concerned with historical accuracy and more inspired by my clients' readiness for lacquer and unexpected color combinations. We amassed a collection of handsome twentieth-century furniture, and I designed the upholstery and laid out schemes that I knew would keep the interior vibrant and cheery, an escape from the hectic city many floors below.

The entry hall was reimagined with complex prewar details in a deep rich blue for added contrast.

The lacquered library has a private terrace and views of Park Avenue. FOLLOWING SPREAD: Hints of gold and parchment in the black-and-charcoal dining room create an intimate setting for dinner parties.

ABOVE: The family room is adjacent to the kitchen and has a cozy breakfast nook in the corner.
OPPOSITE AND FOLLOWING SPREAD: The large abstract painting in the living room is by Helen Frankenthaler from 1987. PAGES 62-63: In lieu of art, panels of dyed parchment adorn the fireplace wall, making way for the strong black sculpture by Louise Nevelson to the right. The club chairs are by Léon and Maurice Jallot, France, 1948.

ASTOR SUITE
THE PLAZA HOTEL

NEW YORK CITY

In the entrance hall, large eglomise inset panels reflect light from the living room windows. A nineteenth-century Irish shipbuilder's chair looks sculptural against an eglomise panel. A bleached oak console adds warmth to the otherwise cool environment. FOLLOWING SPREAD: The living room has majestic Central Park views. The antiques and textiles add to the layering and patina, creating the illusion of age.

Antique mantels give authentic spirit to the newly built rooms. The paneling was meticulously measured to ensure that it felt original to the apartment; layers of glaze were applied to create a patina that would otherwise take generations to attain.

The 1940s French oak table and a leather banquette provide additional seating for casual dinner parties. ABOVE: The leather-clad kitchen door was inspired by a trip to Blenheim Palace, where I was lucky enough to visit the private quarters.

The Plaza Hotel, built in 1907 in French Renaissance château style, was partially converted into large apartments in 2008. The building is revered as a rich surviving relic of old Manhattan, and my European clients decided it would make for a perfect New York City pied-à-terre. The building has a rich patina and a grand monumental scale that one would more likely find abroad. Unfortunately, when the apartment was converted from the famous Astor Suite into a large three-bedroom unit, all of the original details and architectural elements were demolished. Only bland rooms with park views remained. We settled on the notion of redesigning the apartment to suggest rooms frozen in time, as if creating a congenial stage set. I wanted the new interiors to convey that vintage atmosphere, so every surface was artfully distressed to suggest years of use and the softness that comes from decades of exposure to sunlight and layers of wax.

We commissioned millworkers to create paneled rooms and specialty painters to add layers of transparent colors, which were then lightly sanded, glazed, and waxed. The paneling was configured using the proportions of antique rooms I had measured in France, and the plaster ceilings in the dining room were adorned with elaborate cast tracery. All of the ceilings were skim coated and waxed to catch the light in uneven, characterful ways. The English oak library and doors throughout were crafted in Oxford, England, then shipped in large crates to New York, where they were reassembled, much like ornate rooms from Europe were transplanted to Fifth Avenue mansions during America's gilded age.

For the decor, I introduced heavy Belgian and Italian linens and silk velvets in complex, subtle, and nearly neutral colors. We acquired furniture in Europe and America, purposely combining worn eighteenth-century leather chairs, eighteenth-century Italian cabinets, twentieth-century French desks and tables, and midcentury abstract art. This assemblage of rugged textiles, casual and timeworn, along with the various pieces of furniture and art, seems timeless, relevant, and modern.

The oak library has a vintage desk by Jean-Charles Moreux and a custom Chesterfield sofa.

A curtained bed gives the master bedroom a luxe vibe, and the heavy Belgian linen keeps it young and modern.

Coffee is served on the round table at the end of the bed, with a banquette and armchairs fireside.

MORTON STREET
TOWNHOUSE

NEW YORK CITY

The nineteenth-century facade was repointed and cleaned. I designed a new cornice and added shutters, which had been absent for nearly a century. OPPOSITE: Interior architectural details were custom built to complement the few remaining original elements, including the floors and staircase.

Morton Street, in the West Village, is delightfully quirky and curves midway (a rarity in New York City). It is lined with big old trees and mostly nineteenth-century townhouses and apartment buildings that feel charming and friendly. In 2011 I purchased a townhouse that had belonged to a well-known artist for four decades. The building had been chopped up into four apartments. I was moving from a nearby townhouse that I had completely rebuilt due to structural issues; this time I was determined to retain as much of the original structure as possible. While removing later additions we uncovered the old floors, which sagged and sloped to an alarming degree. Instead of rebuilding to gain level floors, I decided to accept and exaggerate the eccentric remaining features. The greatest challenges involved lowering the kitchen floor by three feet, opening access to the garden, and replacing the roof and windows. I designed new doors, casings, millwork, and cabinetry to conjure the illusion of timeless West Village character. I was eager to incorporate some of my favorite artworks and furniture from my previous townhouse and reimagined a design scheme to blend them into our new life on Morton Street.

During the renovation, my husband, James, and I traveled to Austria and visited several museums lined with early dark religious paintings. I wasn't particularly interested in their devotional topics, but I loved their deep black, oily-textured canvases; only a shadow of their subject matter was visible through centuries of oil, grime, and aged varnish. I knew this was the surface I wanted for the library walls. Replicating it ultimately proved to be an arduous task for several painters. While the renovations were under way, we traveled in search of the unusual and amassed a collection that now feels like an integral part of this historic house.

OPPOSITE AND FOLLOWING SPREAD: My West Village living room is a composition of favorite objects.

The oxblood and pink library glows at night and welcomes guests in from the entry hall. The bar is set up, and drinks are served while coats are put away in the guest closet. The nineteenth-century mantel was found in France.

PREVIOUS SPREAD: During renovations, the kitchen floor was lowered by three feet to gain ceiling height and access to the garden. ABOVE AND OPPOSITE: The custom cabinetry and shelves display hotel silver and everyday dishes. The kitchen sink was inspired by a house in Amsterdam; it incorporates an antique faucet found on a European expedition. FOLLOWING SPREAD: The vintage vitrine displays old hotel silver and antique basalt Wedgwood. The plaster mantel is a mannerist interpretation of an English original.

PREVIOUS SPREAD: The black library was inspired by the sheen of Old Master paintings. The firebox was rebuilt to accommodate a nineteenth-century French mantel. ABOVE: The carved eagle is an eighteenth-century Italian lectern. OPPOSITE: The large contemporary bird painting is by Maria Kozak. FOLLOWING SPREAD: The two guest rooms have serene individual personalities.

I added a skylight at the top of the staircase for extra light; it supports an Italian octagonal lantern suspended from a three-story chain. The art is a collection of paintings from the New Hague School of the late 1950s. The Italian cabinet is by Gio Ponti.
ABOVE: Two small powder rooms are tucked away and treated as odd visual surprises.

In the master bathroom, the graphic juxtaposition of two contrasting marbles exemplifies one of my signature themes when designing bathrooms. The nineteenth-century Belgian safe and antique white glazed eagle came from my previous townhouse.

The master bedroom, with a large north-facing skylight, was formerly an artist's studio. The chest of drawers and mirror are eighteenth-century Italian, found on a buying trip in Parma. OPPOSITE: The marble-topped bedside table is eighteenth-century Irish, and the chair is by T. H. Robsjohn-Gibbings. A 1960s painting by André Brasilier depicts sport horses, a favorite subject of my husband, James.

A SWISS VILLA

ZURICH

My notion of the ideal project is one in which I am involved in every detail from the very beginning and one that is imbued with history and strong vernacular ties to a unique region. Two of my favorite longtime clients purchased a spectacular property in Zürichberg, a historic district east of Zurich with amazing views of the city, the dome of the Kreuzkirche Zürich-Hottingen, and Lake Zurich. The villa was built in 1925. We carefully preserved the character of the building, but the entire structure was rebuilt in order to comply with new building codes and alleviate any issues with hillside moisture seeping into the foundation. This afforded the opportunity to introduce elaborate technology, a lower level to accommodate an indoor pool, a garage to display an impressive car collection, and entertaining space.

Working closely with my clients, we compiled images of regional architectural details along with pictures and dimensions of the original villa for design inspiration. We were also determined to retain the terracotta roof tiles and to use as many reclaimed materials as possible to ensure that the final house would have the strong presence and patina of the 1920s villa. We used fragments of eighteenth-century paneling to obtain the perfect proportions for cabinetry and installed nineteenth-century parquet floors originally from the Palais Garnier opera house in Paris. I found a pair of handsome nineteenth-century mantels in Philadelphia, carved out of King of Prussia marble, and installed one in each of the primary living rooms. I am fascinated by the paradox that these mantels have traveled vast distances yet seem perfectly in place in this new setting.

Details adhere to classical principles, but the villa's plan is entirely designed around my clients' lifestyle. They always want casual areas for lounging and reading, and feel the very best views and spaces should be used for daily activities, not reserved for entertaining. In lieu of a formal dining room, a long banquette and rugged table provide a sumptuous setting for hearty dinners. Comfortable deep sofas among sturdy antiques set a relaxed tone.

This handsome villa is entirely new, but attention to historical details, including vintage roof tiles, gives it an authentic feel.

Floors in the front hall were made of antique reclaimed stone. The staircase was built with fumed English oak by Symm in Oxford, England. OPPOSITE: A detail of the hallway's architectural embellishments. FOLLOWING SPREAD: The main living room highlights one of a pair of antique mantels from Philadelphia.

One of the main public rooms features a black stone worktable. My clients believe that the best rooms in the house should be enjoyed by the family, not solely reserved for entertaining. The large portrait of King Leopold is by Andy Warhol. FOLLOWING SPREAD: An intimate corner in the oak library works well for small dinner parties.

The master bedroom was built from wired English oak with upholstered hand-blocked panels.
OPPOSITE: The orange closet doors were crackle-glazed to achieve an aged effect.

PREVIOUS SPREAD, LEFT: Hallways highlight antique oak floors and dry fumed oak millwork. PREVIOUS SPREAD, RIGHT, AND ABOVE: Beams and planks in the kitchen were reclaimed from a demolished barn and sourced locally by the cabinetmaker. Walls were clad in glazed black Moroccan tiles; floors were set with large slabs of Petit Granite from Belgium. OPPOSITE: The informal dining room has a long banquette and views into the kitchen. The high-gloss black beams and trim were inspired by multiple trips to Amsterdam and evoke the graphic quality of historic Dutch interiors.

MAYFAIR APARTMENT

LONDON

I invariably find fresh inspiration in every project, but the prospect becomes especially exciting when it aligns with my current creative obsessions. In Mayfair, London, a couple I had recently worked with asked me to design a pied-à-terre in a historic, listed building. Its interiors had been previously gutted by a developer and modernized to appeal to an exclusive market, but none of the new surfaces or floor plans held any allure for us. The apartment's elegant proportions had been disguised under dropped ceilings, the finishes were slick, and technology was evident on nearly every surface. My clients agreed to demolish almost all of the newfangled changes. In doing so we were able to restore the old ceiling heights and design a new floor plan with proper relationships between rooms.

The surrounding Mayfair architecture inspired my design scheme for the interiors. Every window in the apartment offered views of its classical language, mixed with peculiarly animated Victorian blocks and later twentieth-century buildings with elegant art deco detailing. I was intrigued by the textures and multiple shades of mocha and greige in the limestone coursing and by the warm, brownish-yellow hue of the London stock brick. Accordingly, the walls of the new entrance gallery are rough-coat plaster with a taupe finish. The detailing eliminates any cornice or casing and relies instead on thick raised panels to emulate masonry construction. The pinkish-gray Fior di Pesco marble floor is bordered with a band of dark Grigio Carnico marble, a combination that reflects the juxtaposition of materials of the buildings outside the adjacent window. The tall overdoors in inset plaster were based on doorframes at the Villa Empain, an early 1930s art deco house in Brussels. Bronze doors with inset embossed leather have the same luster and weightiness as the entrance gallery materials, but the warmth of the leather panels segues nicely into the furnished rooms.

The public spaces feel decidedly warmer, but nearly every surface has patina, texture, and "rugged polish," which became our mantra while working on this project. Walls in the snuggery are upholstered in mossy green velvet, which draws one into its comfort and sets the tone for cozy London pied-à-terre living.

Entrance gallery walls are rough-coat plaster; thick raised panels emulate masonry construction.

Texture rather than color creates architectural interest in the entry. The custom designed console, made of pitted travertine limestone, is part of the assemblage of "rugged polish."

The office bathroom plays off an unusual red marble that seems very "London" in its saturated color and combines handsomely with bronze. The eighteenth-century English mirror feels modern in its irreverent setting. FOLLOWING SPREAD: Off the entrance hall, the dining room establishes the mood for the public spaces.

PREVIOUS SPREAD AND THIS SPREAD: The living room is layered with oyster waxed plaster and black Venetian plaster to create a fitting background for the custom pitted quartzite mantel, the grouping of unusual twentieth-century furniture, and British art. FOLLOWING SPREAD: The moss green velvet snuggery is framed by the living room doors and almost appears to be a painting on the wall, rather than a room to enter.

The art is hung salon style to enhance the intimate feel of this cozy space.

The kitchen's palette is derived from the heavily grained Calacatta Paonazzo marble counters and floors, which are muted by black and charcoal accents and texture on every surface.

Walls in the master bedroom are inset with bands of silk wall covering whose colors were inspired by the semiprecious stone mantel, custom made in India for the firebox. Curved corners in the room reference some of the unusual architectural details discovered while exploring Mayfair.

The master bedroom's orientation was reconfigured to optimize views of the picturesque eighteenth-century streetscape outside. The dressing room is rendered in English oak with velvet-lined cubbies and a generous built-in window seat.

The master bathroom was meticulously assembled using two types of marble: remarkable book-matched slabs of Cipollino Verde Ondulato bordered with contrasting bands of dark Verde St. Denis for visual impact. Bronze hardware, doors, and plumbing fittings add to the room's masculine feeling.

Hand-painted silk walls in the office evoke a moody landscape punctuated by splashes of red. The large custom vitrine grounds the room and displays a collection of oddities.

COUNTRY

A FAMILY HOUSE
IN WATER MILL

NEW YORK

When envisioning the plans for a newly constructed compound on Mecox Bay, the design team looked farther afield than the traditional local shingle style. The massing of the buildings suggested more of a village layout, so that is what we decided on. Working with the architecture firm Historical Concepts, we reimagined a twentieth-century house made to appear as if parts had been added and adapted over time. The clients' creative verve assured us that an artistic assemblage of vintage components, collaged together much like a village in the Cotswolds, would be charming, atmospheric, and set the right tone. We requested several mock-ups of masonry and rough-sawn timbers, bleached and limewashed and scrubbed to imperfection. Indoors, we used rough-coat plaster, textured patchwork marbles, and hefty timbers in Dutch high-gloss ebony and raw oxidized oak. The wide fumed oak plank floors were cerused and rubbed down with wax.

The overall palette of the textiles and painted surfaces was inspired by the delightful artistic personalities of the owners and by the irreverent assemblage of objects and furnishings I found to embellish the interiors. I have always admired the way the Bloomsbury group of twentieth-century English artists decorated their sixteenth-century farmhouse, Charleston, in Sussex, England. It proclaims their abiding belief in the importance of all the arts, yet is comfortable and relaxed. In Water Mill, my goal was to establish a similar feeling that was also thoroughly modern and reflected the family's sensibilities. Unusual color combinations and abstracted patterns were threaded together, establishing uniformity but also hinting at intriguing discoveries to be found around each corner. The large Naturalists Room furthered this sense of adventure; glass vitrines envelop the room with collections distilled from nature.

The mudroom serves as the primary entrance for the family.

PREVIOUS SPREAD AND THIS SPREAD: The Great Hall welcomes friends and family and also serves as a giant dining room for entertaining. The quirky spirit of mismatched candlesticks and artworks in the Great Hall sets the tone for an unmistakably artful home for a creative family.

The large living room is on axis with the front door and provides sweeping views of Mecox Bay.
FOLLOWING SPREAD: The elongated sofa highlights a grid of drawings by Joseph La Piana.

PREVIOUS SPREAD AND THIS SPREAD: The library is a composition of eclectic patterns and color combinations.

In the Naturalists Room, a sculptural, tangled root is displayed on the mantel and reflected in the large eglomise panel. The room has a series of glass-encased vitrines backed in antiqued mirror; they are styled with fragments found in the woods, along beaches, and on trips abroad.

The guest wing has its own entrance, made of simple wooden planks. ABOVE: In a guest room, the scheme of pale grays and plum browns relies more on pattern than color for visual impact.

A guest room. ABOVE: The master bedroom feels tucked in under deep eaves with its planked and beamed ceilings and panels of warm bark wallpaper. A pair of doors opens onto a sleeping porch with views of the gardens, pool, lawn, and Mecox Bay.

The breakfast room further exhibits a fascination with nature and the unexpected. The tree trunk table base was salvaged and artfully silver leafed. The vintage light fixture came from a 1950s movie theater. FOLLOWING SPREAD: The large family kitchen celebrates exotic stone and is punctuated with blasts of orange.

A FAMILY COMPOUND
IN BRIDGEHAMPTON

NEW YORK

Working with Historical Concepts is always a creative journey among like-minded architects. On the porch, brick columns were inspired by those built for Thomas Jefferson at the University of Virginia. The brick was parged in plaster and limewashed, adding depth and age to the newly constructed house. The informal front entrance hall sets the tone for casual family living.

A close-knit family had grown, and now three generations shared a vacation house near the ocean. Their goal was to build an even larger compound where everyone could vacation together, poolside, and unwind amid seemingly infinite farmland views. I was hired as the project's overall design visionary, but the superb team was vast and included a contractor, landscape architects, structural engineers, and architects. We chose once again to work with Historical Concepts, known for their smart massing of major structures, and their ability to establish a "village" of smaller buildings to accommodate multiple purposes while respecting the landscape. The look of the new house is decidedly Hamptons vernacular with enough familiar elements to feel as if it has evolved over time. Subtle shifts of muted colors along with traditional materials, such as parged brick and clapboard, help reduce the scale and add casual ease to the meandering facades.

Within the structure, generously proportioned rooms are architecturally detailed with simple casings and wide-planked floors, and layered with warm textures and glazed painted finishes so that no surface stands out as too crisp or too sharp. They have a subtle, earthy vibe, and only the endless landscapes seen through the windows draw your attention away from the cozy indoor spaces.

A hallway vignette. FOLLOWING SPREAD: Three substantial tables in the large dining hall can be quickly reconfigured into one for twenty guests.

PREVIOUS TWO SPREADS: In the living room, an abundance of nubby, soft, luxurious textures in silk and linen feels laid back and inviting. The walls were hand painted to look like driftwood. OPPOSITE AND ABOVE: The Field Room, designed for large evening gatherings, has two game tables. The Kaare Klint red chairs and Gio Ponti sconces add a mellow tone to the carefully composed scheme.

PREVIOUS TWO SPREADS: The kitchen has ample workspace but is mostly used for casual family lunches. OPPOSITE: The painting in the breakfast room is by Robert Dash, a local artist known for his Madoo Conservancy. ABOVE: The large butler's pantry is more of a servery, where meals can be laid out buffet style. It connects the family kitchen and the chef's kitchen, enabling efficient service and easy access to large supplies of dishes and cutlery.

A back staircase leads from the large mudroom up to the house's private living quarters. ABOVE: The mudroom design is intentionally simple with a "back of house" feeling; it is durable and suitably rugged for dogs, luggage, and sports equipment.

The master dressing room is paneled with wired and cerused oak. OPPOSITE: The spacious upper hall landing separates the master suite from a series of guest bedrooms. FOLLOWING SPREAD, LEFT: The upstairs gallery has a high-gloss barrel-vaulted ceiling. FOLLOWING SPREAD, RIGHT: A small office for the owner has views of verdant fields, which inspired the room's vibrant color palette.

OVERTON HOUSE
IN SAG HARBOR

NEW YORK

The upstairs landing is artfully arranged with found objects. OPPOSITE: The house's nineteenth-century door surround was faithfully restored; the front door was replaced with a Dutch door for light and air circulation.

Sag Harbor, on the East End of Long Island, has long been one of my favorite places. I am fascinated by the village's complex architectural and social history; what began as a small seaside port and community grew and prospered during the eighteenth and nineteenth centuries, when fortunes were made in the local shipping and whaling industries. Many of the town's finer homes have prominent architectural details built by craftsmen engaged as shipbuilders nearby. Certain elements, like stair railings, become mini research projects as I try to identify their original cabinetmakers.

I had often admired the Overton House, even though it had been divided into apartments and looked rather dilapidated. The proportions of the old structure and the beautiful doorframe remained, albeit buried within a poorly clad exterior and obscured by unfortunate later additions. When the house became available, I bought it to extend my creative projects in Sag Harbor, which now include six personal renovation projects and several others for clients and friends.

From the beginning, my goal for the Overton house was to add new wings while retaining everything of historic value. I also wanted to experiment with first-rate craftsmen using the best materials. At a time when the fragile village was undergoing enormous change, with a surge in popularity and a rash of new development, I wanted my renovation to be an eloquent visual statement about the degree to which historic dwellings should be scrutinized and appreciated. After all, each contributes to the charm of these streetscapes, so cherished for their authenticity.

The interior architectural features are an encyclopedia of vernacular details I have gathered and incorporated into multiple village renovations. Each proportion is local to Sag Harbor, down to the plank dimensions, casing profiles, and plaster crowns. There are also elements I have established as my own vocabulary. It has been rewarding to incorporate many of these favorite components into the "best of" under one roof.

The original staircase and railing are highlights of the entry; the newly designed Dutch door opens onto the historic village streetscape.

Furnished as a reception room, the main entrance hall has a large eighteenth-century Swedish table adorned with a collection of antique stone mortars. The raised paneling is adapted from historic examples but is more elaborate than this house would have ever had.

The mudroom entrance leads from the gravel driveway for easy access to cabinets and closets for informal summer living. Planks of painted wood, Dutch doors, waxed antique pine floors, and large brass rim locks are some of my favorite architectural elements.

Handsomely proportioned halls allow for vignettes and tablescapes that give visual interest to transitional spaces.

The serving pantry is a visual display for dishes. It is also a coffee station and a bar, out of the way of the kitchen. A wall of restoration glass panels lets natural light filter through the center of the house.

This back staircase leads from the kitchen to the upper quarters, providing easy access from the master bedroom for morning coffee. A rich blue service door leads to the dining room. ABOVE: The kitchen's Dutch door is on axis with the front door to encourage cross breezes.

Pale gray marble is used for the countertops and deep stone sinks in the kitchen. A nineteenth-century English farm table is paired with vintage chairs by Milo Baughman.

In the square dining room, a nineteenth-century English cabinet displays vintage books, china, and various curiosities.

A corner of the dining room. ABOVE: The round dining room table serves as a stage set for tabletop vignettes.
FOLLOWING TWO SPREADS: The front parlor in the original nineteenth-century section of the house.

The double-height Great Room is in the new part of the house. FOLLOWING SPREAD: One of three seating areas in the Great Room.

This thirteen-foot-long vintage mural of sailors and masts travels with me to various projects and houses. FOLLOWING SPREAD: Details of the master bedroom.

The nineteenth-century stone foundation had to be rebuilt, so we decided to dig below the original house to create a new basement. The wine room displays bottles on simple stone shelves, much like the storehouses found in early American houses. Stone floors were custom cut to match the proportions of ballasts used on ships in the port during the nineteenth century.

EAST HAMPTON
GUESTHOUSE

NEW YORK

ABOVE AND FOLLOWING SPREAD: This deep summer porch shields guests from the sun and offers a comfortable place to relax and view the grounds and gardens beyond. OPPOSITE: Quirky objects and lighting in the front entrance hall set the tone.

In East Hampton, after partaking in a very large reconstruction of an ocean-front estate, the family grew to need a separate guest compound with space for ample entertaining. The guesthouse is affiliated with a staff house, garage complex, chicken coop, organic garden, and tennis court; it is also an ideal location for big gatherings. The clients engaged my firm to work with Historical Concepts as the lead architects and Nelson Byrd Woltz as the landscape architects, and as a team we developed the program, sequence of spaces, and overall appearance of the compound. The clients asked us to suppress the scale to make the buildings appear understated as a series of auxiliary structures on a classic New England estate.

This project called for a series of guest bedrooms for visiting families, separated into two connected wings with shared public areas in between. The vernacular was derived from local wooden houses, where planks of wood and simply dressed interiors keep things from feeling too precious or refined. The exterior is decidedly classical but with spare, pragmatic detailing, and is painted charcoal gray to blend with the landscape. Inside, singular personalities were devised for each bedroom, offering variety for returning guests. Antiques with peculiar forms or details were sourced stateside and abroad, for a collected spirit. We designed deep sofas and selected textiles for their texture and re-strained palette. In the library, which also serves as a dining room, the walls and ceiling were clad with marbled bookbinding paper. In the kitchen, we installed Arabescato Orobico marble counters and cabinets with reclaimed violet-tinted glass panels and a large industrial light fixture for unexpected oddity and visual strength.

The lower guest hall serves as a sitting room and coffee station.

In the master bathroom, a grid of paneled walls is a theme I reference often for its simplicity and graphic impact.

PREVIOUS SPREAD AND OPPOSITE: Paneling in the master bedroom was inspired by a visit to a historic colonial revival house by Delano & Aldrich. I was fascinated by the raised paneled ceiling and had to give it a try myself.

The double-height drawing room was designed for large gatherings. Three triple-pane windows open up to become portals, leading to the gardens beyond.

The dining room doubles as a reference library; the walls and ceiling are clad with marbled bookbinding paper.

The guest kitchen is moody and rugged, with vintage industrial lighting and a hammered gun-metal hood. Marble counters have been weathered to add to the overall effect of timeworn surfaces.

Each guest bedroom has a unique color story. FOLLOWING SPREAD, LEFT: The upper guest hall has four Greek mattresses to accommodate visiting children. FOLLOWING SPREAD, RIGHT: A captain's bed.

LITTLE GLOVER
IN SAG HARBOR

NEW YORK

The antique garden gate is a reclaimed stall door from a horse stable. The house is newly built, but its proportions are true to the historic nineteenth-century village houses of Sag Harbor.

Sag Harbor's architectural appeal is more about its nineteenth-century streets-capes than about individual structures. Each building plays a role in the overall character, and I think it is critical to work within the vernacular of the simple wooden houses that line the charming village lanes. On Glover Street, a small house of a later date was not in keeping with the saltbox purity of the sur-rounding buildings and was structurally unsound. I purchased the site, which is visible from my primary village house, and proceeded to design a cottage. With Historical Concepts, I studied the massing and setbacks required for the Architectural Review Board, but generally it was an easy process because I was eager to create a house that would blend in with handsome neighboring structures.

As the house developed it was dubbed "Little Glover" and became a bit of a laboratory for some of my latest architectural and design interests. I sketched rooms that would require specialty millwork and stonework and began collecting reclaimed materials as a starting point for the design process. I purchased the pine paneling of an eighteenth-century room from a house in Salem, Massachu-setts, which had been acquired by a museum and deaccessioned in the 1930s. I designed a room large enough to reinstall the paneling, along with several ad-ditional walls of new panels and trim to match the eighteenth-century originals. I worked with a very accomplished craftsman, William Suchite, who was equally enthusiastic about the challenge; his skill and ingenuity further influenced my use of complex details. We would meet at the house and I would draw directly onto the unfinished walls. He would then build mock-ups of the proportions until we were satisfied with the results. This on-site process was a refreshing departure from office projects that require multiple sets of drawings and workshop diagrams before construction.

The organic vegetable garden. FOLLOWING SPREAD: The elaborate front door, transom, and sur-round were often added to simple early Sag Harbor houses after a successful whaling expedition. I have always thought the contrast seemed uniquely "Sag Harbor" and decided to play up that architectural feature.

The front parlor has rough-coat plaster walls and a simple mantel made from ancient marble. ABOVE: The oddly shaped stone object was found on a buying trip in France, and rests on a stone base found locally.

Little Glover evolved one room at a time and soon took on a distinct personality. I was more inspired by stories of sea captains returning from expeditions with newfound wealth and inspiration to build their dream houses than with specific features from local interiors. Little Glover was to be my version of a travelogue, filled with the simple details that I sketch when visiting historic houses. The paneling for the large sitting room was completely built by William, based mainly on my sketches of eighteenth-century paneled rooms in Virginia. We studied books and photographs but were more intent on capturing the essence of how such details were interpreted in rural settings of the period. The simplicity of the room makes it feel more authentic, and the atmosphere seems entirely real. While visiting my stone fabricators' warehouses and stone yards, I came across remnants of the marble facade of a demolished Fifth Avenue mansion built at the beginning of the twentieth century. The giant carved columns, cornices, and blocks of stone were beautifully worn from a century of decay. I selected fragments of the egg-and-dart cornice, which were recut into an oddly scaled bolection to frame the oversize firebox. The combined play of scale and materials seems the perfect backdrop for the spare collection of my favorite furniture, arranged with deliberate irreverence.

Pine paneling from an eighteenth-century room in Salem, Massachusetts, was installed in the dining room. FOLLOWING SPREAD: Irreverent details in the kitchen suggest age.

Our breakfast room has a large built-in vitrine full of oddities collected over the years. Light streams through the Dutch door on the front of the house, which faces west. OPPOSITE: Sailor, our labradoodle, observes the day's activities from the best seat in the room.

The back room will soon become my studio for painting and creative projects. This curious collection of furniture consists of some favorites that needed a room worthy of their display. The walls are finished in layers of gently sanded and waxed limewash. FOLLOWING SPREAD: This upstairs hallway leads to a series of guest bedrooms.

Steven Gambrel is founder and president of S.R. Gambrel, Inc., a New York City interior design/architecture firm that also produces custom furnishings. His international projects have been featured in such leading publications as the *World of Interiors*, *Architectural Digest*, *House Beautiful*, *Elle Decor*, and the *New York Times*. Gambrel's first book, *Steven Gambrel: Time and Place*, was a bestseller.

ACKNOWLEDGMENTS

I would like to thank my incredible office staff for their keen focus and constant support. Every member of my team brings an individual expertise to each project, and their combined efforts make our success possible. I am especially grateful to Oscar Molina for assisting me in *Perspective*'s art direction of photography, and to Elizabeth Stanton for overseeing so many administrative duties.

I thank Rizzoli's Publisher, Charles Miers, and Senior Editor Sandy Gilbert Freidus for encouraging me to publish my second book with Rizzoli. To Sandy for overseeing the varied elements of *Perspective*: you have my deepest gratitude for your attention to detail. Thank you to Rizzoli's marketing, sales, and publicity staff members for bringing my work to a wider audience.

Thank you Christopher Mason for helping me to express so clearly the nuances of my process. Your outstanding talent and friendship are invaluable. And my thanks to Sara Pozefsky for assisting Christopher in refining my words.

Mary Shanahan, a special thanks to you for your incredible ability to present my work on these pages in a way that reflects my sensibility.

Collaboration has always been a key aspect of my practice and is deeply rewarding. Thank you to the contractors and architects who make these projects come to life.

And, finally, to my clients, who continue to trust my perspective on design. Your support and enthusiasm are what it's all about.

—STEVEN GAMBREL

ARCHITECTURE AND CONTRACTING CREDITS

Palmolive Building Apartment, Chicago
Architect: Phillip Liederbach, Liederbach & Graham Architects, LLC
Contractor: Bulley & Andrews, LLC

Fifth Avenue Duplex, New York City
Architect: Arcologica, Ltd.
Contractor: S. Donadic, Inc., Construction Management

Park Avenue Prewar, New York City
Architect: Gary Brewer of Robert A. M. Stern Architects, LLP
Contractor: Interior Management, Inc.

Astor Suite, The Plaza Hotel, New York City
Architect: Arcologica, Ltd.
Contractor: McGraime Interiors

Morton Street Townhouse, New York City
Architectural Consulting: S.R. Gambrel, Inc.
Contractor: SMI Construction Management, Inc.

A Swiss Villa, Zurich
Architect: Cyrill Mathis of Mathis Meier Architects, AG

Mayfair Apartment, London
Architectural Consulting: S.R. Gambrel, Inc.
Contractor: Damian Segal Property Renovations

A Family House in Water Mill, New York
Architect: Historical Concepts
Contractor: Seascape Partners, LLC

A Family Compound in Bridgehampton, New York
Architect: Historical Concepts
Contractor: Michael Davis Construction, Inc.

Overton House in Sag Harbor, New York
Architect: S.R. Gambrel, Inc., in collaboration with Historical Concepts
Contractor: Timeless Homes, Ltd.

East Hampton Guesthouse, New York
Architect: Historical Concepts
Contractor: Bulgin & Associates, Inc.

Little Glover in Sag Harbor, New York
Architectural Consulting: S.R. Gambrel, Inc.
Contractor: Timeless Homes, Ltd.

First published in the United States of America in 2018 by
Rizzoli International Publications, Inc.
300 Park Avenue South
New York, New York 10010
www.rizzoliusa.com

2018 2019 2020 2021/10 9 8 7 6 5 4 3 2 1

Printed in Italy

ISBN 13: 978-0-8478-6324-2

Library of Congress Control Number: 2018946274

Project Editor: Sandra Gilbert
Production Editor: Maria Pia Gramaglia
Editorial assistance provided by Sara Pozefsky,
Kelli Rae Patton, and Megan Conway
Design Consultant: Mary Shanahan